To my son, Johnny—the most perfectly imperfect ten-year-old. Never let age or time stop you from daring greatly.

Carolrhoda Books®
An imprint of Lerner Publishing Group, Inc.
241 First Avenue North
Minneapolis, MN 55401 USA

For reading levels and more information, look up this title at www.lernerbooks.com.

Main body text set in Avenir LT Pro 65 medium.
Typeface provided by Linotype AG.
The illustrations in this book were created with mixed media.

Library of Congress Cataloging-in-Publication Data

Names: Beccia, Carlyn, author. | Beccia, Carlyn, illustrator.
Title: 10 at 10 : the surprising childhoods of ten remarkable people / Carlyn Beccia, Carlyn Beccia.
Other titles: Ten at ten
Description: Minneapolis : Carolrhoda Books, [2021] | Audience: Ages 8–12 | Audience: Grades 4–6 | Summary: "At age ten, Audrey Hepburn evaded the Nazis. What was Roberto Clemente doing at that age? Or Albert Einstein? Lively text and striking illustrations present some of history's most famous figures in a whole new light" —Provided by publisher.
Identifiers: LCCN 2020057691 (print) | LCCN 2020057692 (ebook) | ISBN 9781541545007 | ISBN 9781728417431 (ebook)
Subjects: LCSH: Children—Biography—Juvenile literature.
Classification: LCC CT107 .B424 2021 (print) | LCC CT107 (ebook) | DDC 920.0083—dc23

LC record available at https://lccn.loc.gov/2020057691
LC ebook record available at https://lccn.loc.gov/2020057692

Manufactured in the United States of America
1-45466-39692-10/29/2021

# 10 AT 10

## THE SURPRISING CHILDHOODS OF TEN REMARKABLE PEOPLE

CARLYN BECCIA

Carolrhoda Books

Minneapolis

# TABLE OF CONTENTS

# INTRODUCTION

It's not easy being ten. There are things to learn, rules to follow, teachers to impress, friends to make, bullies to avoid, and your body is about to get weird on you.

Ten is an important year because you have survived what psychologists call the formative years. That's just a fancy way of saying your personality has started to take shape. But you are not done. Think of yourself as a lump of clay. In the next ten years, your personality will squish and squash in ways that may surprise you and everyone around you. It will get molded and formed before it hardens into something magnificent.

Take for example Albert Einstein. At the age of ten, did Einstein know he would someday come up with the theory of relativity? Hardly. At ten he was your typical smart kid with a lot of questions rolling around his head and an attitude that annoyed most of his teachers. How about Louis Armstrong? If you could peer into a magic looking glass and see his life at ten, you would likely not have predicted that he would become a world-class jazz musician. Then

there is ten-year-old Audrey Hepburn, who barely made it out of war-torn Holland alive, and Frida Kahlo, who had polio as a kid and went on to create art that would speak to people across the world.

Bruce Lee spent his tenth year fighting on rooftops, getting terrible grades, and tormenting his teachers. After his formative years, he matured and started to see things differently. He then began filling up notebooks with his life philosophies. Later he wrote, "All knowledge ultimately means self-knowledge." What Bruce meant is that knowing yourself is the most important step in gaining outside knowledge. You can't begin to understand others until you understand yourself. This is called self-awareness.

None of the people in this book knew what path they were on at the age of ten. They were all ordinary kids with everyday hopes and fears. And it's really hard to be ourselves when we don't fully know ourselves yet. That's why we look to role models to figure it out. They are our brave guides who light our path. I hope the following stories of courage and perseverance will inspire you.

# ZITKÁLA-ŠÁ

## 1876–1938

As a young girl, Zitkála-Šá spent her time leaping and bounding over rolling hills and past the rising smoke of her home on the reservation in Yankton, South Dakota. When she stopped, the scene stopped. When she jumped, it jumped. No matter how fast she ran, she was a part of the land.

When she was eight years old, Quaker missionaries visited to recruit Native children to the White's Indiana Manual Labor Institute in Wabash, Indiana. At first, she was excited to go. The white people promised to take her away on an "iron horse" (a train) to lands where she could eat "big red apples" and learn to read and write.

Her mother warned her, "Their words are sweet, but, my child, their deeds are bitter." Her mother had good reason to be distrusting. Years earlier, gold had been discovered in the Black Hills of the Dakota Territory and prospectors took over lands belonging to Dakota, Lakota, and Northern Arapaho people. During that same time period, US leaders such as President Ulysses S. Grant encouraged killing bison as a way to eliminate Native Americans because they were dependent on the animals for meat, clothing, and utensils. And Indigenous people were also being coerced into signing treaties, forced onto reservations, and required to adopt farming instead of hunting and gathering.

By the time missionaries arrived to take Zitkála-Šá away, the landscape where thirty million bison had roamed had been reduced to herds of just five hundred and the Yankton Western Dakota people had been forced to leave their ancestral lands as protectors of the Pipestone Quarry.

Her mother's warning proved correct. When she arrived at her new school, all the apple trees had died.

And so Zitkála-Šá began her new life with new clothing, a new language, and a new name—Gertrude. She would

**1876**
Zitkála-Šá is born.

**Age 8**
Attends White's Indiana Manual Labor Institute

Missionaries cut off her hair.

**Age 11**
Returns to the Yankton Reservation but feels like she has lost her culture

**Age 14**

Between 250 and 300 Lakota Indians die at the Wounded Knee Massacre.

**Age 20**

Wins second prize in the Indiana State Oratorical Contest

**Age 21**

Studies violin at the New England Conservatory of Music

**Age 25**

Publishes *Old Indian Legends*

**Age 34**

Helps compose the first Native American opera, *The Sun Dance*

later describe the school as an "iron routine" filled with the monotony of ringing bells and roll calls. The white people who ran the schools considered Native people to be savage, and their punishments were intended to erase the children's Native culture and language. Those punishments were harsh and swift. If children spoke in their native language instead of English, they were forced to stand on tiptoes with arms outstretched for over an hour. Other punishments were meant to embarrass. If a child wet the bed, they carried the bedroll with them all day.

Shortly after her arrival and fearing the eyes of the white women, Zitkála-Šá hid under the bed and listened to the sound of sharp footsteps coming closer and closer. Suddenly, rough hands pulled her from her hiding place. She kicked and screamed and then felt the cold steel of a scissors against her neck. Her long braids were chopped off one by one.

Zitkála-Šá would later say that was the day she lost her spirit. In her culture, only cowards or mourners had their hair shorn. Zitkála-Šá was neither.

When Zitkála-Šá was eleven years old, she returned home, but she was caught between two worlds—her old life as a proud Dakota and her new life in the white world. She felt she was "neither a wild Indian nor a tame one." Zitkála-Šá lamented, "Like a slender tree, I have been uprooted from my mother, nature and God." With her people being pushed out of their lands, the roots she planted would have to be in the new world.

She returned to school and was lauded for her oratory skills and musical talents and as a perfect example of a reformed Indigenous person. But the shadow of her lost heritage clung to her, and she became determined to show that side to the world. In one of her speeches, "Side by Side," delivered at the age of twenty, Zitkála-Šá's stirring words showed the injustices of a "cold race whose hearts were frozen hard with prejudice."

As an adult, she fought for equal rights for her people and challenged the practices of American Indian boarding schools. At the time, Native Americans were denied American citizenship and could not vote. Many lived in poverty without enough food, water, or sanitation. Still, the US government had continued to seize lands and break treaties that promised protection from white settlers taking over Native lands. When Zitkála-Šá was fourteen, roughly 250 to 300 Lakota were killed at the Wounded Knee Massacre.

Zitkála-Šá saw these injustices and decided the only way to fight them was to continue her education. She was awarded a scholarship to attend Earlham College in Indiana where she began to collect and write down stories from Native tribes. She worked hard to portray her people as seeking to stand side by side with fellow Americans. She published stories in *Atlantic Monthly* criticizing boarding schools that ripped children from their families and forced them to adopt the religion, language, and culture of white society without giving them the same rights.

One of the ways she protected Indigenous culture was through music and dance. Zitkála-Šá teamed up with white composer William F. Hanson to write *The Sun Dance Opera*, the first known Native American opera. The opera featured a sacred dance, and actors dressed in authentic costumes. This was a bold move. At the time, ceremonial dances were outlawed by the American government. But Zitkála-Šá knew that art could build a bridge between her people and white ideals.

Politics became the other bridge. In 1926 Zitkála-Šá and her husband founded the National Council of American Indians. One of the primary goals was to obtain the right to vote. Although Native Americans were granted citizenship in 1924 through the Indian Citizenship Act, the US Constitution left it up to the states to decide who had the right to vote. Many states continued to deny voting rights to Native Americans for the next forty years.

Zitkála-Šá died in 1938 before she got to see her dream of equal rights for her people or the elimination of Native boarding schools, but her writing remains in the hearts of Native American people today.

**Age 40**
Becomes secretary of the Society of American Indians

**Age 44**
Publishes American Indian Stories

**Age 47**
Exposes the ill treatment of Native American tribes in Oklahoma's *Poor Rich Indians*

**Age 50**
With her husband, forms the National Council of American Indians (NCAI)

**Age 61**
Dies

$P = \frac{mv}{\sqrt{1-v^2/c^2}}$
E=MC²
A² + B²=C²
SIN X
COS X
SPEED OF LIGHT=299792458 M/S
mc² - moc²
$y^1 = y$
$z^1 = z$
$t = t$
$\Delta M = \frac{\Delta E_0}{c^2}$
a²
b²
c²

# ALBERT EINSTEIN

## 1879–1955

There is this rumor about Albert Einstein. Maybe you have heard it? It goes something like this: Einstein is considered one of the most brilliant scientists in the last century, but at ten years old, he got horrible grades. So horrible that his teachers didn't particularly care for him.

One part of this rumor is true. Albert's teachers did dislike him. But not because of his grades. They disliked him because he was always correcting the teacher, constantly asking questions, and often not bothering to do the homework because it was too easy for him. Albert actually got very good grades in school, but teachers often lost patience with him because he would take too long to answer questions. The problem was that schools at the time focused on rote memorization of facts instead of seeing patterns in events and understanding why they happen. Albert could think in pictures but struggled with words, and he didn't want to blindly memorize facts without understanding them. We call this conceptual thinking, but Albert would have called it using his brain.

To get by, Albert sat in the back of the class and just smiled at his "drill sergeants" when he failed to get an answer correct. This, of course, only annoyed his teachers more. His Greek teacher told him he would never amount to anything. His math teacher called him a "lazy dog."

One time, he got kicked out of class because, according to his teacher, his mere presence destroyed, "the respect which a teacher needs from his class."

In his neighborhood in Munich, Germany, Albert was the weird kid on the block. He didn't even speak until the age of three, and when he finally did speak, he skipped right to full sentences. At ten, he would often wander the streets of

**1879**
Albert is born with a BIG head

but an average-sized brain.

1,230 grams
(weight of his adult brain)

**Age 2**
Doesn't talk

?    •••

**Age 4**
Father gives him a compass.

Likes to play alone

Age **5**

Throws a chair at his teacher

Age **10**

Is not the teacher's pet

Age **12**

Meets Max Talmud, who gives him books

Discovers love of physics

Munich alone, and while most boys his age played sports, he preferred to do puzzles or build a fourteen-story house of cards. If the card house fell, he would build it again. And again. And again.

His closest friend was his younger sister, Maja, probably because she learned to give Albert the space he needed to daydream. She learned this the hard way when her big brother threw a bowling ball at her head. Maja later dryly observed, "It takes a sound skull to be the sister of an intellectual."

Albert at ten was spirited, stubborn, aloof, and far too clever for his own good. When a subject interested him, he applied himself 100 percent, and when it didn't . . . he slacked off. Like most kids with a lot of potential, he needed someone to steer him in the right direction. That someone was a friend of the family's named Max Talmud. Realizing that Albert was gifted in conceptual thinking, Talmud brought Albert volumes of books on physics, geometry, philosophy, and algebra. Albert devoured science fiction books with "breathless attention."

Still, Albert's advanced aptitude for science and math didn't always open doors for him. When he was sixteen, he failed his university entrance exam. Not because it was too hard but because he didn't bother to study for the history or language portion. (And, yes, even if you're Einstein, you have to study.) Thankfully, when he retook the exam, he passed it.

After graduating in 1900, Albert struggled to get a job. He was certainly smart enough but was also a bit of a know-it-all. He often corrected other teachers' work, and that didn't win him any friends. One professor warned Albert: "You have one fault. You won't let anyone tell you a thing."

That professor was right. Albert believed the most important thing in life was not to stop questioning. He conducted "thought experiments" where he visualized the answer through pictures. From these thought experiments, Albert realized that gravity doesn't push an object in a straight line like an apple falling from a tree but, instead, moves objects through space and time on a curve. He then theorized that how much energy an object had was in proportion to its mass—the quantity of matter, or stuff, in an object. This thinking led to his most famous equation: $E=mc^2$.

Scientists at the time believed all levels of energy had been discovered, but Albert knew to look deeper. He once said, "[We] never cease to stand like curious children before the great mystery into which we were born."

Einstein also questioned the repressive Nazi Germany government that sent Jewish people, like Einstein, to concentration camps. In 1933, It was rumored that Nazi agents were trying to assassinate Einstein. In response to these rumors, Einstein renounced his German citizenship and fled to England and later to the US. In the US, he spoke out against Nazi Germany.

Whether it was politics or science, Albert was never afraid to speak his mind. He accomplished so much because he never stopped being that annoying, questioning ten-year-old kid determined to find the answer . . . his own way.

"The important thing is not to stop questioning."

$$E = mc^2$$

Age 15
Masters calculus

REPORT CARD
MATH      A
SCIENCE   A
GREEK     F
HISTORY   F

Age 16
But fails his entrance exam

Age 21
Graduates

Questions Newton

Age 26
Writes theory of relativity

Age 42
Wins Nobel Peace Prize

Age 76
Dies

# LOUIS ARMSTRONG

## 1901–1971

As a boy, Louis Armstrong would walk barefoot along Jane Alley in New Orleans, Louisiana, past rows of crude wooden shacks with peeling paint and past the criminals hanging from the scaffold by the parish prison. New Orleans was segregated—Black people and other people of color were not allowed to live in the same neighborhoods, attend the same schools, eat at the same restaurants, or even use the same bathrooms as white people.

Louis was born in 1901 in a district of New Orleans called Storyville. This area bustled with so much gambling, drinking, and crime that it became known as the battlefield. On every corner, music streamed out of dance halls called honky-tonks, bars known for their cheap booze and bawdy entertainment. Once Louis reached the music hall, Funky Butt, he would press his ear against a crack in the wall to hear feet stomping on wooden floors, shuffling madly to keep up with the frenzied ragtime, a style of music that would later evolve into jazz. Through tiny peepholes, seven-year-old Louis would watch the tall, slim cornet player Buddy Bolden, known as King Bolden, take the stage and play his horn so loudly that people claimed he could be heard across "14 miles [23 km] on a clear night."

When the hour got too late, Louis walked home to the red bean and rice dinner waiting for him in a one-story, two-room house in Storyville. Louis's dad had left when Louis was a baby, and his mom struggled to make ends meet. To earn extra money, Louis would entertain passersby on street corners by drumming on a soapbox with a stick or whistling through his fingers to imitate the horned melodies he heard at Funky Butt. But it was Louis's antics that earned him showers of pennies. He would close his eyes and roll them backward in mock ecstasy and finish with a big smile. Louis's smile was

**1901**
Louis is born.

**Age 9**
Is arrested for stealing scrap metal

**Age 11**
Is arrested again for shooting a gun

**Age 12**
Sent to:

Discovers music

COLORED WAIF'S HOME

**Age 12**
Buys his first
used cornet

**Age 17**
Joins the
Kid Ory band

**Age 21**
Switches to playing
trumpet

Makes his
first recording

**Age 23**
Joins the Fletcher
Henderson Orchestra

so wide that his friends called him "Satchel mouth." The name was later shortened to Satchmo, a nickname he would use throughout his life.

Happiness was easy for Louis. Keeping out of trouble was not. When Louis was nine, he was arrested for stealing scrap metal to resell to junkyards, and he dropped out of school the following year. When he was eleven, he was arrested again for a more serious charge—firing a pistol on New Year's Eve. He was sentenced to the Colored Waif's Home for Boys, a reform school surrounded by barbed wire and run like a military camp. Louis would later say it was the "greatest thing that ever happen to me" because it forced him to shape up and find his salvation—music. At the school, he played the tambourine and then the bugle, but it was his first cornet that made him play so hard that he split his lip on several occasions.

He was released by the Waif's Home eighteen months later and hired to play in a local honky-tonk at just fourteen years old. By the time he was fifteen, one of the greatest cornet players, Joe "King" Oliver, began tutoring him. By 1922 Oliver sent for Louis to come to Chicago and be his second cornetist for his Creole Jazz Band. But it was not long before the student surpassed the teacher, and in 1924 Louis joined the Fletcher Henderson Orchestra in New York.

In New York, Louis became popular for his unique style that told a story through music. He would often start off performances with his back to the crowd, hang his head, and then spin around to blow with perfect tone until he reached a heart-pounding climax. He played such earsplitting high notes that musicians accused him of sticking chewing gum into his horn—an old trick to hit high notes. Sometimes between blowing he would scat—interjecting nonsense syllables with his gravelly voice. Then he would mop his brow with the white handkerchief he always kept on him, put his horn back to his lips, and jump back into the song.

Louis did not invent jazz, but he instilled jazz with his lively personality.

Jazz would evolve into swing and then bebop in the '30s and '40s. In later years, jazz record sales would dwindle as the

British band the Beatles took over the charts. But despite the public's dwindling interest in jazz, Louis never changed his style. Through it all, Louis continued to have the support of fans. When he was sixty-three, he became the oldest artist to hit number one on the pop charts with his hit, "Hello, Dolly!" One interviewer asked him if musicians of the past played more "from the heart."

He replied, "If it sounded good, I don't care where it came from . . . music is music."

That was who Louis was. He hated when musicians "put on airs." Louis hardly ever complained, and he had plenty to complain about. One racist radio announcer refused to introduce him because of the color of his skin, and when he toured, he sometimes had to sleep on the bus because Black people were not allowed in most hotels. Louis would later say, "I made the best, the very best of an awful situation."

Louis was also outspoken when necessary, especially when it came to civil rights. When Arkansas governor Orval Faubus tried to prevent nine Black students from integrating a Little Rock High School in 1959, Louis spoke out against segregation and called Faubus, "no good" (among other things). In response, many Americans boycotted his records. Louis did not care. He was going to speak his mind. He was the first jazz musician to write his autobiography and could often be found at his typewriter, clicking away writing chatty letters to his friends riddled with dramatic ellipses and signed cheekily, "Red Beans and Ricely Yours, Louis Armstrong."

When Louis blew, he did not blow for the pain of his past or his hopes for the future. He blew for the present. He blew for happiness, because to him . . . jazz was happiness.

**Age 24**
Forms
the Hot Five

**1930s**
Jazz declines in favor of swing.

**Age 35**
Becomes the first Black American to get featured billing in a Hollywood film

**Age 56**
Speaks out against segregation in schools

**Age 63**
Releases "Hello, Dolly!"

**Age 69**
Dies

# FRIDA KAHLO

## 1907-1954

You have probably heard the art advice to paint or draw what you see. But what if all you can see is limited to what surrounds your bed? This was the reality Frida Kahlo faced after a bus accident confined her to her bed for over a year. So, Frida chose to paint the most fascinating subject contained in the four walls of her room—herself.

Painting yourself is called a self-portrait, and Frida painted a lot of self-portraits throughout her life. When asked why, she said, "Because I am the subject I know best." Like most artists, Frida was on a quest to know herself through her art, and she held nothing back.

That journey began in 1907 in La Casa Azul—a bright blue house surrounded by a garden of lush tropical plants and the rainbow-colored birds native to Coyoacán, Mexico. Yet despite her surroundings, color did not always fill Frida's childhood. At the age of six she contracted polio, and it left her with one leg shorter than the other. The kids teased her at school and called her peg-leg Frida. She ignored the taunts and filled her days climbing trees and racing around town on her bike.

When she was ten, her father taught her photography—developing, retouching, and coloring photographs. She most likely got her love of surface details from these early art lessons.

When she was fifteen, Frida secured a spot at the National Preparatory School with only twenty-five girls out of two thousand students. Although intelligent, Frida was also a troublemaker. She joined a gang of rebellious kids called Los Cachuchas, named after the cloth caps they wore. The gang discussed politics, culture, and books while pranking teachers. One of the people Frida pranked was the famed painter Diego Rivera. While he was painting a mural at her school, she stole his lunch and soaped the stairs to make him fall.

**1907**
Frida is born.

**Age 3**
Mexican Revolution begins.

**Age 6**
Contracts polio. Her leg shrinks.

**Age 15**
Attends the National Preparatory School to study medicine

**Age 15**
Pranks Diego Rivera by soaping the stairs and stealing his lunch

**Age 18**
Bus accident

**Age 19**
Begins painting from her bed

**Age 21**
Joins the Communist Party

**Age 22**
Marries Diego

Frida's carefree childhood was darkened again when a tram crashed into the bus she was on in 1925. She was impaled by one of the bus railings and suffered a broken spinal column, pelvis, collarbone, rib cage, leg, and a crushed foot. Her injuries were so severe that her doctors didn't know if she would survive. Frida's parents built her a special easel so she could paint lying down and installed a mirror above her bed so she could create her first self-portraits.

After the accident, she slowly regained her ability to walk. During this time, Frida and Diego Rivera fell in love and were married. Diego towered over Frida, and her mother described it as a marriage between an "elephant and a dove." It wasn't just physical size that set them apart. Diego painted grandiose murals that spanned entire walls, while Frida painted intricate portraits the size of a coffee-table book. At the time, few women earned their living as painters, so Frida painted mainly as a way to journal her life and express her views about love, politics, and culture.

Frida traveled with Diego to the US in 1930 but was not happy in America. To start, he often neglected her for his art (or to have affairs with other women). Adding to her despair, Frida became pregnant several times, but all her pregnancies ended in miscarriages as a result of the bus accident that injured her pelvis. Frida painted the loss of her children in several of her paintings. One painting, *Henry Ford Hospital*, depicts her miscarriage in a graphic and disturbing work of art. That raw emotion is one of the things that made Frida's art so unique and is why people were drawn to it.

In 1938 Frida had her first exhibition in New York City. Yet even as she was receiving recognition for her art, her marriage was coming to an end. In the following years, she cut off her hair, threw herself into her work, and decided she would survive without Diego. But it wasn't just her love life that was causing her tremendous pain. Her injuries became worse, and she had over thirty surgeries to fix her spine and leg. Most of the operations made her condition worse. Eventually, her right leg had to be amputated.

Frida had always accepted her injuries, but losing her leg brought on a depression seen in her paintings. Her careful brushwork was replaced by careless energy that was most likely due to the painkillers she was on. In one passage of her diary, she wrote, "I tried to drown my sorrows, but [they] learned how to swim." Frida died from a pulmonary embolism shortly after the amputation of her leg. She was just forty-seven years old.

When you look at a painting you like, it almost always makes you feel strong emotions—joy, despair, anger, fear, peace. Most people are drawn to Frida's paintings because they are ripe with emotion. The last painting Frida painted before she died expressed this ripeness. It is of bright, red watermelons and inscribed with the words, "Viva la Vida" (live life), a fitting title for a woman whose life was short in years but long in experience.

VIVA LA VIDA

**Age 23**
Moves to the US

**Age 26**
Returns to Mexico

**Age 30**
First painting exhibit in Mexico

**Age 46**
Leg is amputated.

**Age 47**
Dies

# EUGENIE CLARK

## 1922-2015

*"Come on in the water . . ."*

So begins one of the scariest scenes in movie history. In Martha's Vineyard, a young girl named Chrissie jumps into the ocean for an evening swim.

Suddenly, something pulls her under. The music thumps like a fearful heart. Seconds pass. She screams, and then all is quiet. The orange glow of dusk dances over the still water.

We later learn Chrissie was attacked by a 25-foot (7.6 m) great white shark set on getting revenge. This is the opening scene of *Jaws*, a movie adaptation of the best-selling novel by Peter Benchley.

Eugenie Clark, a Japanese American researcher and ichthyologist (a scientist who studies fish), hated *Jaws*. Known as the shark lady, Eugenie worked her entire adult life to dispel the public's fear of sharks, and *Jaws* made that mission very difficult. To start, sharks are not interested in revenge, and when they hunt for food, humans are not on the menu. In fact, fatal shark attacks are so uncommon that your odds of being killed by a falling cow are greater. Sharks kill fewer than eighty-four people per year worldwide, and great white sharks account for only five to ten of those deaths.

Eugenie understood a shark's personality better than most because she spent her life around them. Eugenie learned to swim before the age of two. When she was nine years old, her mom would drop her off at the old New York Aquarium while she went to work. Eugenie's father had died when she was two, and with little money for childcare, the aquarium became Eugenie's babysitter. With her face pressed against the cold glass tank, she would imagine herself swimming with the sharks and walking along the seafloor like a weightless ballerina.

**1922**
Eugenie is born.

**Age 2**
Learns to swim

**Age 9**
Visits NYC aquarium. Sees sharks for the first time.

**Age 24**
Receives master's degree in zoology and learns to dive

**Age 28**
Earns her PhD from New York University

Age 31

Writes her memoir, *Lady with a Spear*

Age 36

Teaches lemon sharks to push a button, showing they can learn

Age 37

Discovers belted sandfish

Age 45

Establishes Mote Marine Laboratory

Age 46

Teaches marine biology at the University of Maryland

Those trips to the aquarium led to more questions, and Eugenie became determined to find the answers. She wanted to know what makes blowfish puff out and why the *Triodon* fish has a huge flap of skin descending off its belly. (Both are used to scare off predators.) By the time she was ten, Eugenie became determined to swim with sharks and other fish and to learn everything about their world. Unfortunately, women did not typically become ichthyologists at the time. Instead, Eugenie was encouraged to learn typing so she might become a researcher's secretary. But Eugenie wasn't interested in being a researcher's secretary. She wanted to be the researcher.

Her big break came in 1955 when she was asked by the wealthy Vanderbilt family to start the Cape Haze Marine Laboratory. At her lab, she caught sharks and created a shark pen where she could observe their behavior.

When not in her lab, Eugenie explored the ocean depths to get the answers she craved. She made seventy-two submersible dives, even one as deep as 12,000 feet (3,658 m). Dives at a depth greater than 100 feet (30.6 m) can cause dangerous nitrogen narcosis, a condition in which nitrogen is absorbed by the brain causing a loss of consciousness. But Eugenie never feared the water. She rode on the back of nurse sharks, 50-foot (15 m) whale sharks, and turtles. She braved the depths of the Warm Mineral Springs in Florida with sinkholes so dark that she had to hold a flashlight over the depth gauge on her wrist to see it. In the pitch-black water, she bumped into the skeletons of those who never made it back to the surface of the water. One time, she found a human skull underwater with a fully preserved brain that was roughly 7,140 to 7,580 years old.

Eugenie's research changed what we formerly believed about sharks and other fishes. She found "sleeping" sharks suspended in caves, which busted the myth that sharks need to keep moving to breathe. She also proved that sharks could learn. At the time, it was believed that sharks lacked the intelligence to learn simple tasks such as pressing a button to get food in the same way mice did. Eugenie had no problem teaching her lemon sharks to push a bull's eye with their noses to get a food reward. By studying how her sharks interacted with the different-colored targets, she learned that sharks see in contrast, not color. (This might make you think twice about wearing a yellow-and-black swimsuit in shark-infested waters.)

She discovered the Red Sea sand diver (*Trichonotus nikii*), which she named after her son Nikolas, and the Red Sea Moses sole (*Pardachirus marmoratus*), which releases a natural shark repellent. Eugenie's biographer, José Castro, said that Eugenie had "three qualities that are necessary to be a good scientist: curiosity, education and determination," Not even age could slow Eugenie down. She continued to go deep-sea diving into her nineties until her death at ninety-two from lung cancer.

Eugenie chose to understand sharks instead of fearing them. She said, "come on in the water" to all the shark researchers who would follow her brave strokes.

**Age 47**

Publishes her second book, *The Lady and the Sharks*

**Age 59**

Takes her first ride on the back of a whale shark

**Age 92**

Makes her last dive

**Age 92**

Dies

# AUDREY HEPBURN

## 1929-1993

In the movie *Funny Face*, actress Audrey Hepburn struts across a dimly lit nightclub in a black outfit with a wide-eyed grin. To the clash of cymbals, she bounds atop chairs and tables like a newborn colt that has just discovered its legs. Watching her dance with such grace and contagious joy, it becomes easy to overlook the amount of bloodshed Audrey saw before the age of sixteen.

It becomes easy to forget she almost didn't survive her childhood.

Audrey Kathleen Ruston was born in Brussels, Belgium, to an English father and Dutch mother. By the time she was four years old, Adolf Hitler came to power in Germany. Hitler was a charismatic leader who brought so much economic prosperity to Germany that he was even named *Time* magazine's Man of the Year in 1938. When Hitler's army paraded through the streets of Brussels, Audrey's mother, Baroness Ella van Heemstra, described him as, "one of the most inspiring sights on earth." Little did she know that this inspiring leader's deep-seated hatred toward Jews and other groups would lead to the murder of six million Jews as well as millions of others.

In 1939 Audrey celebrated her tenth birthday while living in England. That same year, Hitler invaded Poland, which began World War II. Her mother feared England would be attacked so they hastily moved to Arnhem, Netherlands, reasoning that Hitler would never attack neutral Netherlands.

While living in the Netherlands, Audrey's family did not have much money. In addition, Audrey struggled to learn the Dutch language while classmates made fun of her English accent. Despite being told she was too tall, Audrey fell in love with ballet and dreamed of becoming a prima ballerina. That dream would have to be put on hold. Six days after she turned

**1929**
Audrey is born.

Audrey gets whooping cough, and her heart stops. Her mom saves her.

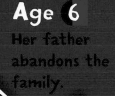

**Age 6**
Her father abandons the family.

**Age 10**
England declares war on Germany.

**Age 11**
Is sent to Holland for her safety

Germany invades Holland.

eleven, her mother burst into her room with the news that would bring Audrey into her darkest days.

"Wake up" she screamed. "The war is on."

That morning war planes sliced through picturesque skies while the sound of wailing sirens came closer and closer. Children pressed their hands against shaking windowpanes as bombs exploded around them. Families gathered around their radios, horrified to hear the words they thought they would never here—Germany had invaded Holland.

Life became very different for eleven-year-old Audrey during the war. Citizens were ordered to stay in their houses as Hitler's police force, sometimes called the Green Police, roamed the streets watching everyone and only allowing pro-Nazi radio shows. Bread rations were reduced and butter, margarine, fats, and creams were gone from Audrey's diet because Germany needed them to feed Hitler's war machine.

Always courageous, Audrey joined the Dutch Resistance, which fought back against Nazi invasion by organizing strikes, helping down enemy planes and, most importantly, hiding Jews. During this time, Audrey saw her Jewish friends rounded up into cattle trucks and taken away to concentration camps. Their terrified eyes were often the last sight she saw of them. To help support those in hiding, Audrey carried hidden messages in her shoes past the watchful eyes of the Nazi Green Police, often risking her own life. To raise money, she gave "blackout" dance performances—secret shows in basements with darkened windows where audiences were not allowed to clap for fear of being discovered.

About an hour's drive from where Audrey lived, a dark-haired Jewish girl the same age as Audrey was hiding in a secret annex in Amsterdam. Her name was Anne Frank, and her family had gone into hiding in 1942. Anne's greatest company was her diary where she wrote to an imaginary friend named Kitty. Anne's hiding place was eventually discovered, and she died in a concentration camp, but her diary lived on. On one fragile and worn page dated May 4 (Audrey's birthday), Anne scrawled the words, "Five hostages shot today." It was a passage that would haunt Audrey later in life after Anne's diary was published. Audrey's beloved uncle, Otto van Limburg Stirum, was one of the hostages executed on that day.

Two years later, Audrey and her mom moved 3 miles (4.8 km) from Arnhem to Velp where her family risked their lives to hide a British soldier. As the war continued, people began to starve. During the Hunger Winter, about five hundred Dutch citizens died each week due to starvation. Audrey was forced to eat flour made from tulip bulbs to survive and had to stop dancing due to malnutrition and anemia—a deficiency in iron due to her poor diet. In one interview, Audrey said of her war years, "You dreamed what would happen if you ever got out. You swore you would never complain about anything again."

Relief came in 1945 when the Netherlands was liberated by Canadian Allied forces. After the war, Audrey moved to Amsterdam to continue dancing and took small acting roles to make ends meet. Although dance would always be her first love, it was acting that catapulted her into stardom. She got her first starring role in the box office success, *Roman Holiday* (1953), and would use her dancing skills in *Funny Face* (1957). Audrey would go on to win two Golden Globe Awards and the Cecil B. DeMille Award. Later in life, she dedicated herself to raising her two sons and her work as a UNICEF Goodwill Ambassador helping to get food to starving children.

In 1959 Audrey was asked to play the role of Anne Frank. She turned it down, perhaps because she did not want to revisit the trauma from her war years. In one interview she said, "The past, I think, has helped me appreciate the present." Audrey moved beyond her past childhood tragedies—dancing, acting, giving to others, and living her life to the fullest.

**Age 25**
Stars in *Sabrina*

**Age 28**
Uses her dancing skills in *Funny Face*

**Age 31**
Stars in *Breakfast at Tiffany's*. The movie makes her a fashion icon.

**Age 59**
Serves as Goodwill Ambassador for UNICEF

**Age 64**
Dies

# ROBERTO CLEMENTE

## 1934–1972

Roberto Clemente always stepped up to the plate the same way. Eyes down, he rotated his neck side to side and kicked the ground with his foot. When he lifted his head, fans knew he was ready. With one graceful swing of his ridiculously heavy bat, he lifted his rear foot off the ground and . . . CRACK.

"That one is going . . . and it is GONE!" the 1971 Major League Baseball All-Star Game announcer proclaimed over the roar of fans.

Roberto once said, "You are playing for people who pay to see you. You are giving entertainment to people." Between his odd batting technique, his sliding catches slamming into walls, and his spinning throws from right field, entertain he did. Everything Roberto did was a kaleidoscope of dramatic acts.

The first act began in his childhood. As a boy in his hometown of Carolina, Puerto Rico, Roberto always had clothes on his back and food to eat but few luxuries. The people of Carolina drank rainwater collected in boxes and rode mules, horses, or bicycles to work. For ten cents, Roberto could take a bus to the local ball games, but he often did not have the fifteen cents to get in so he would climb a tall tree and watch the ant-sized players from above.

Whatever Roberto lacked was filled with his love for one thing—baseball. As a ten-year-old, he practiced with the neighborhood kids on muddy fields hidden under the shade of palm trees until it was too dark to see. With little money for equipment, he sculpted bats out of hard guava tree branches and made a glove out of an old coffee bean sack. For a ball, he hit anything he could find—bottle caps, twine rolled up into a ball, crumbled newspapers, or empty soup cans. Roberto would later recall that as a kid he "loved baseball more than anything."

**1934**
Roberto is born.

**Age 10**
Squeezes rubber balls to increase the strength in his hands

**Age 16**
Becomes a track-and-field star

**Age 18**
Is signed by the Brooklyn Dodgers for $10,000

The Dodgers hide him so that he will not get drafted by another team.

## Age 18

Starts for the Montreal Royals

Is the only Puerto Rican player on the team

## Age 20

Is chosen by the Pittsburgh Pirates in the first round of the minor-league draft

## Age 24

Joins the US Marine Corps

## Age 25

The Pittsburgh Pirates win the World Series. Clemente hits .314 with 16 homers and 94 runs batted in.

By the time he was seventeen, a scout from the Brooklyn Dodgers, Al Campanis, had recruited Roberto Clemente calling him, "the greatest natural athlete" he had ever seen. A year later, in 1955, the Dodgers lost Roberto to the Pittsburgh Pirates where he played right field.

But in the US, Roberto struggled to learn English and adapt to US customs. Sportswriters often mocked his English by spelling quotes out phonetically to dramatize his accent. "Me like hot weather, veree hot," they would write. Or "ball" became "bol." This infuriated the proud Roberto.

Other sportswriters cast him in the role as a chronic complainer. In the '50s and '60s, athletes did not talk about injuries, but Roberto spoke openly about his injuries and illnesses and he had a lot—a back injury from a car accident, shoulder and elbow injuries, headaches, stomachaches, malaria, and insomnia. Once when asked how he was feeling, he replied, "My bad shoulder feels good, but my good shoulder feels bad." This was Roberto's way. If you asked him how he was feeling, he was going to tell you.

Roberto often wondered if sportswriters were so hard on him due to the color of his skin. In some parts of the country in the 1950s, Black players were not allowed to stay at the same hotels as white teammates or go to the same movies and beaches. When traveling, he had to stay on the bus because Black players were not allowed to eat at the same restaurants or use the same bathrooms. Sometimes Roberto simply refused to take the bus "if we can't eat where the white players eat."

Perhaps because he was so vocal, Roberto had to work harder to get the credit he deserved. After the Pittsburgh Pirates won the 1960 World Series, Roberto was passed over for the Most Valuable Player award, which was given to teammate Dick Groat. Roberto came in eighth in the voting. If Roberto felt pain from this slight, it only made him more determined. His batting average got better and better, and by the age of thirty-eight he got his three-thousandth hit.

Roberto was driven by pride and by wanting to help others. When he was in Puerto Rico during the off-season, he would carry a bag of coins so he could hand them out to people. While traveling with the Pirates, he would visit sick children in hospitals, and he even donated the money he earned from endorsements to children's hospitals. Despite his busy schedule, he still made time to hold baseball clinics for impoverished kids and dreamt of building a sports city in Puerto Rico to help young players.

Those plans were cut short in 1972. Just before Christmas, a devastating earthquake hit Nicaragua where he coached amateur baseball. Frustrated that food and supplies weren't reaching the people quickly enough, Roberto took action. He found a pilot to charter a DC-7 plane loaded with food and supplies so he could personally deliver them.

Roberto had always had a fear of flying and even told his wife, Vera, and others that he believed he would die young. Vera was worried about the flight. As his plane disappeared over the Atlantic, those fears came true. The plane would never reach its destination. For days afterward, fans stood along the beach praying and throwing petals into the water. The only part of Roberto that washed up was one sock.

Whenever Bob Prince, announcer for the Pirates, had greeted Roberto he shouted, "¡Arriba!, ¡Arriba!," playfully rolling his *r*'s off his tongue. It translates in English as "get there" or "go up," but its roots come from the Latin "to reach the shore."

Roberto Clemente never reached his shore. He never got to accomplish all his dreams. But he did reach so many fans who remember and still love him.

**Age 31**
Named National League Most Valuable Player

**Age 36**
The Pittsburgh Pirates win the World Series.

**Age 38**
Reaches 3,000 career hits

**Age 38**
Dies

**1973**
Becomes the first Latin-born player to be inducted into Baseball's Hall of Fame

# RAVEN WILKINSON

## 1935-2018

On a sweltering afternoon in 1957, a bus carrying Raven Wilkinson and the dancers of Ballet Russe rolled into the sleepy city of Montgomery, Alabama. The tour bus had gone through many segregated southern states, but the greeting from Montgomery was particularly terrifying.

A flock of angry men in white robes swarmed around her bus, stopping traffic. They wore white hoods pointed toward the sky like a church's steeple. Hoods that hid their faces, but not their eyes. Eyes filled with enough hate to do the unthinkable—to hurt Raven because she was Black.

The enraged men were members of the white supremacist group the Ku Klux Klan, or KKK. They had discovered that the Ballet Russe included a Black ballerina, and they were determined to stop Raven from performing. One screaming Klan member jumped on the bus and threw down a bunch of racist pamphlets before being kicked off by the company's male dancers.

That night Raven stayed locked inside her hotel room and was not allowed to perform. Peeking out from her window, she saw a cross burned on the lawn.

This incident was not the first time Raven Wilkinson had to stare down racism. In the late 1950s, Black people in the southern US were not allowed in white schools, theaters, restaurants, or even public restrooms.

Anne Raven Wilkinson was born in 1935 and raised in Harlem, New York. When she was five, she fell in love with ballet after seeing Les Ballets Russes de Monte Carlo perform *Coppélia*—a comic ballet about a doctor who falls in love with a life-sized dancing doll. She was so moved that she sank into her chair and cried.

**1935**
Raven is born.

**Age 5**
Sees her first ballet—Coppélia

**Age 9**
Takes her first ballet lesson

**Age 19**
Auditions for Ballet Russe but is rejected

Age **20**

Becomes the first
Black American
woman to dance
for a major classical
ballet company

Age **26**

Leaves the
Ballet Russe
because
of racial
discrimination.
She does not
dance for
two years.

Age **32**

Joins the Dutch
National Ballet

At nine, her uncle gave her a gift that would change
her life. He paid for lessons at the Swoboda school. Raven
began studying with Russian dance instructor Madame Maria
Swoboda. Raven was the only Black student.

The Swoboda school was eventually bought by Ballet Russe,
and Raven desperately wanted to dance for them. But every
time she auditioned, she was rejected. Finally, a friend at the
school broke the hard truth to her, "Raven, they can't afford to
take you because of your race."

Raven didn't give up and kept on auditioning. By her third
try, she got to see her "dearest dream" come true. She would
become the first Black ballerina to dance with a major classical
ballet company.

There were some conditions. Her instructor told her, "So
you'll tour with us as far as Chicago, and then we'll see."

The "we'll see" part was because the company would be
touring through the segregated South after Chicago, and no
one knew if southerners would accept a Black ballerina.

Raven was forced to wear white makeup and was told to
stand near foreign dancers to look less Black. She was often
asked if she was Black by racist hotel owners. Raven refused
to lie. She refused to deny who she was, even if it interfered
with her dance career.

Montgomery was not the only city that discriminated
against her. Some cities refused to let her stay in their hotel
with other white performers, while other cities demanded they
kick her off the bus and leave her at the side of the road.

It wasn't just racism that kept Raven from living her dream.
Part of the problem Black ballerinas faced then (and still face)
is that classical ballet is viewed as an art where uniformity
prevails. Ballerinas are supposed to be identical, straw-thin
girls with the same skin color. Anyone with a curvier shape
or a different skin tone is still not seen as belonging to that
uniform look.

Raven felt the "disappointment at the limitations that were
placed" on her career and stopped dancing for a few years.
But dancing called her back to the stage, and she eventually
left the US to dance in Holland. In the Netherlands, Raven

danced for the Dutch National Ballet as a second soloist. But seven years later, she missed the United States and decided to return.

At forty years old, she did not intend to go back to dancing, but fate had other plans. She got a call from the ballet master for the New York City Opera, asking her to dance in two of their operas. Those two roles led to more roles and acting jobs. She did not stop dancing until she was fifty, and she enjoyed her acting career until 2011.

In a 2014 interview, Raven was asked about the modern ballet's lack of diversity. She responded with a more pertinent question, "When are we going to get a Swan Queen of a darker hue?"

Raven finally got to see that dream come true in 2015 when Misty Copeland became the first Black principal dancer in American Ballet Theatre's history. Misty credits Raven for being her "hero" because "it was the first time I felt a connection with another ballerina." With tears in her eyes, Misty states her purpose: "To tell the stories of all these Black ballerinas . . . and make Ballet our own."

Raven Wilkinson began that story. Now other dancers, including Misty Copeland, will finish it.

**Age 40**
Returns to the US. Performs as a dancer and actress with the New York City Opera.

**Age 76**
Leaves the New York City Opera when it closes down

**Age 80**
Misty Copeland becomes the first Black American to gain principal status with the American Ballet Theatre (ABT). She credits her hero, Raven Wilkinson.

**Age 83**
Dies

# BRUCE LEE

## 1940-1973

When Bruce Lee was a teen, his kung fu (or gōngfu) teacher, Ip Man, was frustrated with his young student. Bruce attacked with too much focus on winning. His teacher wanted Bruce to calm his mind so he was more in tune with his opponent. Ip Man advised his fiery student, "Remember never to assert yourself against nature." But seeing that his words were not being understood, he told Bruce, "Don't practice this week: Go home and think about it."

And so, Bruce did. That week he went out on a boat to meditate. But while reflecting on his teacher's words, anger swelled up inside him and he began punching the water. That's when Bruce suddenly understood. When he punched the water, it moved out of the way. When he tried to grasp the water, if flowed through his fingers. Water seemed weak because of its softness, but it could penetrate the hardest of substances. Water did not fight against nature but flowed with it.

Bruce realized he must be like water.

This was not an easy lesson. Bruce was born a sickly baby in San Francisco but moved to Hong Kong with his family shortly after his birth. By the age of six, he had been in movies, playing the scrappy punk surviving the rough and tumble streets of Hong Kong. It was a role not far from reality. He was constantly teased by other students at school because he was scrawny and weak with thick, horned-rimmed glasses.

Bruce responded to the taunts by fighting . . . a lot. One of his teachers called him a "devil in the holy water soup" and his constant hyperactivity earned him the nickname Never Sits Still.

One exhausted teacher once sent Bruce to the headmaster with a simple note: "Sending you Bruce to have a few moments of peace."

**1940**
Bruce is born.

**Age 6**
Stars in first major role

**Age 13**
Studies Wing Chun under renowned kung fu master Ip Man

**Age 18**
Wins the Crown Colony Cha-Cha dance competition

Age 19
Leaves Hong Kong to finish school in San Francisco

功夫

Teaches Americans Kung Fu

Age 26
Stars as Kato in The Green Hornet.

Bruce gets more fan mail than even the star.

Age 27
Creates Jeet Kune Do

Age 30
Suffers a back injury while lifting weights

When he was ten years old, Bruce was sent to a secondary school where his English improved, but his attitude got worse. After far too many black eyes, his parents agreed to let him take martial arts lessons so he could learn Wing Chun, a style of close combat kung fu fighting developed by the Buddhist nun Ng Mui.

But as Bruce got more skilled at fighting, he only fought more. Eventually, his brawling got him kicked out of school. Worried that he would never graduate from high school, his parents sent him to San Francisco to finish school at the age of nineteen.

In the US, Bruce graduated from high school and went on to study philosophy and drama at the University of Washington. But instead of applying himself, he poured his passions into teaching Americans kung fu and filling notebook after notebook with his philosophies and extensive diagrams on fighting.

Bruce came up with a name for his style of martial arts—Jeet Kune Do, which translates as "the way of the intercepting fists." He described it as the "art of fighting without fighting." Over the years, Bruce had matured and did not believe in showing off when fighting. He taught his students the art of defense instead of offense. One of his most famous moves was a "one-inch punch," a close distance defensive punch with no windup that sent opponents flying.

Although Bruce's fame as a martial artist grew, he struggled to find acting jobs. During this time, Hollywood rarely gave Asian Americans lead roles. They were usually cast as railroad workers, servants, or villains. Sometimes, if a role called for an Asian actor, studios would dress a white actor as Asian, painting the actor's face and taping their eyes back. Bruce was disgusted by Hollywood's prejudices, and he turned down roles that cast Asians in stereotypical roles.

With US roles scarce and debts mounting, Bruce moved to Hong Kong to pursue acting. His compact 5-foot-7-inch (1.7 m) frame burst into the Hong Kong movie scene with a "Waaataaah," nunchaku flying around him in a blur and a kick so deadly that stunt performers didn't want to work with him for fear of getting hurt. (His kicks literally sent people flying through the air.) Directors even had to ask him to slow down his movements because they were too fast for the camera to capture. Hong Kong fans fell in love.

Hollywood eventually noticed his fame in Hong Kong. Soon Bruce was cast to star in *Enter the Dragon*, and he became the first Chinese man to star in a Hollywood film. At a time when fight scenes were staged and gimmicky, Bruce choreographed his own fight scenes and did his own stunts so that they looked more real. Unfortunately, all that realism took its toll. He lost 20 pounds (9 kg), wasn't sleeping well, and was getting headaches. After one long day of exhausting shooting, Bruce was resting in a friend's apartment and was found unconscious.

Bruce was declared dead on arrival at the hospital. His death to this day remains a mystery. The autopsy report showed his brain had swelled, which is a side effect of heatstroke. However, it also could have been an allergic reaction to pain medicine. He was only thirty-two years old.

*Enter the Dragon* premiered weeks after Bruce's death and grossed US$90 million worldwide. It is still considered to be one of the greatest martial arts films ever created.

In one of Bruce's many notebooks, he wrote, "Discard all thoughts of reward, all hopes of praise and fears of blame, all awareness of one's bodily self . . . let the spirit out, as it will." Bruce never got to see the rewards for his hard work on *Enter the Dragon* nor did he get to collect the praise he deserved for bringing awareness to Taoist and Buddhist philosophies. But his spirit continues to touch lives.

"I fear not the man who has practiced 10,000 kicks once, but I fear the man who has practiced one kick 10,000 times."

武術

43

**Age 31**
Returns to Hong Kong

Stars in
*The Big Boss*

**Age 32**
Stars in Fist of Fury

Returns to US to film *Enter the Dragon*

Dies

# ANDRÉ THE GIANT

## 1946-1993

Most kids know they will someday grow big and tall, but for André René Roussimoff, someday came too soon.

André was born to immigrant farmers in rural Coulommiers, France, on May 19, 1946. He was large at birth (13 pounds, or 5.9 kg), but his brother remembered him as a "normal baby." By ten years old, André's facial features were changing drastically, and he was starting to grow fast. Too fast. By the age of twelve, he had reached a weight of 208 pounds (94 kg) and a height of 6 feet 3 (1.9 m)—4 inches (10 cm) taller than the average full-grown male.

André's incredible size was due to a disease called acromegaly (a-crow-MEG-a-ly), or gigantism, in which too much growth hormone is produced. People who have acromegaly develop larger bones, a protruding lower jaw and brow, and enlarged nose, lips, hands, and feet. Fortunately, André's enormous size had some benefits. When he was eleven years old, one of the wrestlers at his school was hurt and the team asked André to take his place. André said, "I can't do that, I have never been in a ring in my life." But André's size and incredible strength made other wrestlers no match for him. He would throw his opponents over his head as if he were tossing a kitten in the air. When he put his hand over another wrestler's face, his meaty paw was bigger than their head.

The small town of Molien where André grew up could not contain a giant like André. At the age of fourteen, he told his parents, "I don't want to live on a farm all my life. . . . I want to be somebody" so he left home to follow his dreams. By nineteen, he found fame as a professional wrestler named Géant Ferré after a mythical French giant. During this time, André's doctors told him the painful truth—due to his disease,

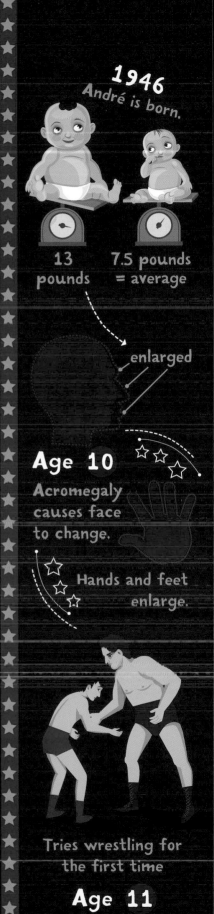

**1946**
André is born.

13 pounds    7.5 pounds = average

enlarged

**Age 10**
Acromegaly causes face to change.

Hands and feet enlarge.

Tries wrestling for the first time

**Age 11**

6ft 3in

**Age 12**

520 lbs

**Age 25**

Is billed as "André the Giant"

**Age 35**

Defeats Killer Khan

he would not live longer than forty. André told no one. Not even his family.

In 1973 André signed with Vince McMahon to join the World Wide Wrestling Federation (WWWF) and was renamed André the Giant. While working for the WWWF, André became the highest-paid wrestler and was billed as the Eighth Wonder of the World. He was advertised as 7 feet 4 (2.2 m), but his real height was closer to 6 feet 10 (2.1 m). His popularity even landed him a role in the cult classic movie *The Princess Bride* as Fezzik, a lovable giant.

André enjoyed his fame but wished he had just one day a week to be a normal size. He had to travel in a special van because he was too large for a car. Plane rides were uncomfortable because he could not fit into the airplane bathroom. And while other famous people could disguise themselves in a baseball cap and dark sunglasses, André stuck out. Everywhere he went, fans gawked and stared. According to wrestling announcer and interviewer "Mean" Gene Okerlund, André had to endure constant teasing and would often cry because of it.

But despite the teasing, André also had a sense of humor. He had a deep guttural laugh, and friends who knew him often took note of his giant smile before even remarking on his giant height. The star of *The Princess Bride*, Cary Elwes, described him as one of "the happiest and most content people" he had ever known. Sometimes he used his incredible strength to play pranks on his friends. He would pick up their cars and move them to face the opposite direction. Other pranks involved his opponents in the ring. After he pinned a wrestler, he would sit on their heads and then let out the longest and foulest fart he could. Jake "the Snake" Roberts remembered André's farts sometimes went on for half a minute. His wrestling opponents knew this about André—if he liked you, he called you "boss" and made you look like a superstar. If he didn't like you, he let you know it with farts and other humiliations.

One of André's friends was wrestling champion Hulk Hogan. On March 29, 1987, André challenged Hogan to the match of the century in a stadium packed with eighty thousand-plus wrestling fans. André entered the ring staring down his opponent and towering over him in a black singlet bodysuit that barely covered his bulging chest. What many fans watching did not know was underneath his bodysuit was a back brace—plates of molded plastic designed to lessen the pain from years of wrestlers pounding on his back.

The match became one of the most famous in wrestling history. Hogan came at André fast, chopping away at his head and neck. André stood solid, as immovable as an old oak tree. Suddenly, André got Hogan in a choke hold, but Hogan turned it around with more chops to André's head. Then, with a lunge off the ropes, Hogan slammed André to the ground to win the match with what became known as "the body slam heard around the world."

André would fight in more matches, but by the late '80s his spine could not support his weight and his knees and back caused him constant pain. André never complained, but he knew his time was running out. André the Giant died a few years later at the age of forty-six from congestive heart failure.

In the small cottage where André grew up, his mom still has her son's kitchen chair, big enough to fit two bottoms. She had it custom built for André so he could sit, and it serves as a reminder of the everyday items that André could not use. André was like an action figure comically placed in a dollhouse too small for him. He lived trapped in a small world in his giant body—a body that eventually put too much stress on his giant heart.

**Age 41**
Stars in *The Princess Bride*

Loses to Hulk Hogan

**Age 42**
Becomes WWE Heavyweight Champion

**Age 46**

Dies

# CONCLUSION

I rarely say this on the last page of any book, but here goes . . . I hope you are thoroughly unimpressed with these ten people. OK, maybe you can admire what they accomplished throughout their lives, but their ten-year-old selves weren't all that extraordinary.

They had to become special.

You might have heard the term *child prodigy*? A child prodigy is a young person who has the same expertise at a certain skill as an adult. Some of the people in this book were called prodigies.

There's only one problem. Child prodigies are extremely rare, and none of the people in this book qualify. Frida Kahlo's art wasn't even fridgeworthy at ten. Louis Armstrong could barely play a single note at ten. And even a young Einstein never contemplated black holes at the tender age of ten. He just wanted to build card houses and tussle with his sister.

All of these greats were pretty average kids when they were ten.

But they shared one common trait—an insatiable hunger to become great. They studied hard, practiced their craft, and worked for what they wanted to achieve. Many had failures and setbacks, but still, they persevered.

On some days, you may wish you could run faster, draw better, or memorize math problems without your head aching. On those days, remember these ten perfectly imperfect ten-year-olds.

# GLOSSARY

**acromegaly:** a disorder in which a person produces too much growth hormone

**All-Star Game:** an annual Major League Baseball game played by top players in the league

**anemia:** a condition in which a person has fewer red blood cells than normal

**aptitude:** natural ability

**bawdy:** indecent in a humorous way

**boarding school:** schools established with the goal of assimilating Indigenous children into white American culture

**boycott:** to refuse to purchase a certain good or service as a protest

**Cecil B. DeMille Award:** an honorary Golden Globe Award recognizing a person's outstanding contributions to the entertainment industry

**charismatic:** having a particular charm or appeal that inspires loyalty or enthusiasm

**charter:** to hire a vehicle for temporary use

**choreograph:** to arrange or direct movements

**concentration camp:** a place where large numbers of people, such as prisoners of war, refugees, or members of an ethnic minority, are detained or confined

**conceptual thinking:** connecting abstract ideas, or concepts, to deepen understanding and create new ideas

**congestive heart failure:** a condition in which the heart cannot pump blood well

**cornet:** a trumpetlike instrument

**discriminate:** to unfairly treat a person or group differently from other people or groups

**endorsement:** an agreement where a person receives money for publicly stating that they like or use a product or service

**Golden Globe Award:** award given by the Hollywood Foreign Press Association recognizing excellence in film and television

**hyperactivity:** the condition of being overly active

**ichthyologist:** a scientist who studies fish

**impoverished:** lacking basic resources or conditions, such as safe housing and access to education and medical care, needed to achieve an equal position in society

**integrate:** to end the segregation of people of different races

**intellectual:** a person of great intelligence who engages in serious study and thought about a topic or topics

**kung fu:** a Chinese martial art practiced for self-defense, exercise, and spiritual growth

**liberate:** to free from domination by a foreign power

**matador:** a bullfighter

**miscarriage:** a condition in which pregnancy ends too early and does not result in the birth of a live baby

**missionary:** a person sent to a place to spread a religious faith

**nitrogen narcosis:** a dangerous state of euphoria and confusion caused when nitrogen enters the bloodstream at increased pressure, as in deep-water diving

**nunchaku:** a Japanese weapon that consists of two sticks joined at their ends by a short length of cord or chain

**oratory:** public speaking

**perseverance:** continued effort to do or achieve something despite difficulties, failure, or opposition

**philosophy:** a field of study focused on knowledge, right and wrong, reasoning, and the value of things

**polio:** a viral disease that causes inflammation of nerve cells in the spinal cord, often accompanied by fever and paralysis

**prejudice:** a feeling of unfair dislike directed against an individual or group because of a particular characteristic, such as race or religion

**premiere:** the first public screening of a film

**prima ballerina:** the principal ballerina in a ballet company

**principal:** a dancer of the highest rank in a ballet company

**pulmonary embolism:** a blockage of one of the pulmonary arteries in the lungs

**Quaker:** a member of a particular Christian denomination

**reform school:** a place where troubled young people were taught, with the intention of improving their behavior and gaining new life skills. Some reform schools were places for young criminal offenders to serve a sentence.

**relativity:** a scientific theory that the way things move through time and space depends on the position and movement of an observer

**salvation:** something that preserves a person from danger or difficulty

**sanitation:** the promotion of good hygiene to prevent disease

**scat:** to improvise nonsense syllables, usually accompanied by music

**segregation:** the forced separation of different racial groups

**soloist:** a dancer in a ballet company that performs minor roles in performances, ranked below a principal dancer

**stereotype:** an often oversimplified or biased representation of a person in a particular group

**submersible:** a small underwater craft used especially for deep-sea research

**theory:** a general rule offered to explain a scientific phenomenon

**UNICEF Goodwill Ambassador:** an official title granted by the United Nations to celebrities, acknowledging their work for children's rights

**uniformity:** having the same manner or appearance

**white supremacy:** the belief that white people are superior to people of other races and should have power over them

# SOURCE NOTES

7   John Little, *The Warrior Within: The Philosophies of Bruce Lee* (New York: Book Sales, 2016), 131.

9   Zitkala-Sa, *American Indian Stories* (Washington, DC: Hayworth, 1921), http://digital.library.upenn.edu/women/zitkala-sa/stories/impressions.html.

9   Zitkala-Sa.

10  Zitkala-Sa.

10  Zitkala-Sa.

10  Zitkala-Sa.

10  Doreen Rappaport, *The Flight of Red Bird: The Life of Zitkala-Sa* (New York: Dial Books, 1997), 60.

13  Peter Smith, *Einstein* (London: Haus, 2005), 13.

13  Michio Kaku, *Einstein's Cosmos: How Albert Einstein's Vision Transformed Our Understanding of Space and Time* (New York: W. W. Norton, 2004), 46.

13  Arthur I. Miller, *Einstein, Picasso: Space, Time, and the Beauty That Causes Havoc* (New York: Basic Books, 2001), 43.

14  Albert Einstein, *The Collected Papers of Albert Einstein* (Princeton, NJ: Princeton University Press, 1987), xviii.

14  Jimena Canales, "Albert Einstein's Sci-Fi Stories," *New Yorker*, November 20, 2015, https://www.newyorker.com/tech/annals-of-technology/albert-einsteins-sci-fi-stories.

14  Patricia Lakin, *Albert Einstein: Genius of the Twentieth Century* (New York: Simon Spotlight, 2005), 20.

14  Sidney Perkowitz, "Gedankenexperiment," *Encyclopædia Britannica*, February 12, 2010, https://www.britannica.com/science/Gedankenexperiment.

15  Walter Isaacson, *Einstein: His Life and Universe* (London: Simon & Schuster UK, 2008), 132.

15  Albert Einstein, *The Ultimate Quotable Einstein* (Princeton, NJ: Princeton University Press, 2013), 425.

17  Terry Teachout, *Pops: A Life of Louis Armstrong* (Boston: Houghton Mifflin Harcourt, 2009), 33–34.

18  Pat McKissack and Fredrick McKissack, *Louis Armstrong: King of Jazz* (Berkeley Heights, NJ: Enslow Elementary, 2013), 21.

18  Teachout, *Pops*, 36.

19  Joel Newsome, *Louis Armstrong: Jazz Musician* (New York: Cavendish Square, 2017), 75.

19  Newsome, 75.

19  Laurence Bergreen, *Louis Armstrong: An Extravagant Life* (New York: Broadway Books, 1997), 125.

19  David Margolick, "When Louis Armstrong Blew His Top," *Little Rock Arkansas Times*, September 28, 2011, https://arktimes.com/news/cover-stories/2011/09/28/when-louis-armstrong-blew-his-top.

19  Ken Ringle, "Red Beans and Ricely Yours," *Washington Post*, March 3, 1977, https://www.washingtonpost.com/archive/lifestyle/1977/03/03/red-beans-and-ricely-yours/7bb6325f-3d6d-41af-b684-e075ad12a661/.

21  Andrea Kettenmann, *Frida Kahlo, 1907–1954: Pain and Passion* (Köhn, Germany: Taschen, 2000), 18.

22  Lissa Jones Johnston and Frida Kahlo, *Frida Kahlo: Painter of Strength* (Mankato, MN: Capstone, 2006), 14.

23  Hayden Herrera, *Frida: The Biography of Frida Kahlo* (London: Bloomsbury, 2018), 147.

25  Peter Benchley and Carl Gottlieb, *Jaws*, produced by Richard D. Zanuck and David Brown, directed by Steven Spielberg (Universal City, CA: Universal Pictures, 1975).

27  Gavin Naylor and Tyler Bowling, "Yearly Worldwide Shark Attack Summary," Florida Museum, last modified January 27, 2021, https://www.floridamuseum.ufl.edu/shark-attacks/yearly-worldwide-summary.

27 "Myth-Busting—5 Common Misconceptions about Great Whites," White Shark Diving Company, last modified January 15, 2018, https://www.sharkcagediving.co.za/myth-busting-5-common-misconceptions-about-great-whites/.

29 Robert Matzen, *Dutch Girl: Audrey Hepburn and World War II* (Pittsburgh: GoodKnight Books, 2019), 19.

30 Matzen, 43.

30 Matzen, 121.

31 Matzen, 227.

31 Melissa Hellstern, *How to Be Lovely: The Audrey Hepburn Way of Life* (New York: Dutton, 2004), 6.

33 "1971 MLB All Star Game Detroit Original NBC Broadcast," YouTube video, 2:11:04, posted by Phenia Films, accessed October 27, 2021, https://www.youtube.com/watch?v=i_DuSLorLpE.

33 David Maraniss, *Clemente: The Passion and Grace of Baseball's Last Hero* (New York: Simon & Schuster, 2007), 234.

33 Maraniss, 22.

34 Steve Wulf, "December 31: ¡Arriba Roberto!," Vault, December 28, 1992, https://vault.si.com/vault/1992/12/28/december-31-arriba-roberto-on-new-years-eve-in-1972-roberto-clemente-undertook-a-mission-of-mercy-his-death-that-night-immortalized-him-as-a-man-greater-than-his-game.

34 Wulf.

34 Maraniss, *Clemente*, 98.

34 "Roberto Walker Clemente," Encylopedia.com, last modified May 17, 2018, https://www.encyclopedia.com/people/sports-and-games/sports-biographies/roberto-walker-clemente.

34 Maraniss, *Clemente*, 148.

35 Maraniss, 89.

38 Chava Pearl Lansky, "Remembering Raven Wilkinson, Trailblazing Ballerina," *Pointe*, December 19, 2018, https://pointemagazine.com/remembering-raven-wilkinson-trailblazing-black-ballerina/.

38 Margaret Fuhrer, "Raven Wilkinson's Extraordinary Life: An Exclusive Interview," *Pointe*, June 1, 2014, https://www.pointemagazine.com/raven-wilkinson-interview-2412812564.html.

38 Fuhrer.

39 Fuhrer.

39 "Misty Copeland, "She Is: Tells the Story of Trailblazing Ballerina Raven Wilkinson," YouTube video, 2:54, posted by The Root, March 11, 2019, https://www.youtube.com/watch?v=D9vKcxlNkq4.

41 Shannon Lee and Sharon Lee, "The Nature of Water," Bruce Lee Podcast, October 10, 2018, https://podcasts.apple.com/us/podcast/119-the-nature-of-water/id1134673435?i=1000422529252.

41 Matthew Polly, *Bruce Lee: A Life* (London: Simon & Schuster, 2019), 75.

41 Polly, 36.

41 Polly, 36.

42 Paul Bowman, *Theorizing Bruce Lee: Film-Fantasy-Fighting-Philosophy* (Amsterdam: Rodopi, 2010), 43.

43 Aksapada, *The Dragon's Wisdom—Bruce Lee Philosophy: 494 Amulets of the Martial Art Legend*, narr. Carl Martens (SP Production, 2020), 5.

43 Aksapada, 45.

45 *Andre the Giant*, dir. Jason Hehir (New York: HBO Sports, 2018).

45 *Andre the Giant*.

45 *Andre the Giant*.

46 Cary Elwes and Joe Layden, *As You Wish: Inconceivable Tales from the Making of* The Princess Bride (New York: Atria, 2014), 125.

47 "The Slam Heard 'Round the World," WWE, March 17, 2008, https://www.wwe.com/inside/listthis/maniamatches/maniamatches4.

# SELECTED BIBLIOGRAPHY

## ZITKÁLA-ŠÁ

Lamberson, Nicole. "Zitkála-Šá: On Creativity, Copyright, and Cultural Empowerment." *Copyright* (blog). Library of Congress, March 31, 2021. https://blogs.loc.gov/copyright /2021/03/zitkla-on-creativity-copyright-and-cultural-empowerment/.

Zitkála-Šá. *American Indian Stories*. New York: Random House Books, 2019.

———. *Dreams and Thunder: Stories, Poems, and the Sun Dance Opera*. Lincoln: University of Nebraska Press, 2005.

———. *Impressions of an Indian Childhood*. Gloucester, UK: Dodo, 2008.

## ALBERT EINSTEIN

Calaprice, Alice, and Trevor Lipscombe. *Albert Einstein: A Biography*. Westport, CT: Greenwood, 2005.

Einstein, Albert. *Dear Professor Einstein: Albert Einstein's Letters to and from Children*. Edited by Alice Calaprice. Amherst, NY: Prometheus Books, 2002.

Einstein, Albert, Anna Beck, and Ann M. Hentschel. *The Collected Papers of Albert Einstein: The Swiss Years, Writings, 1912–1914*. Princeton, NJ: Princeton University Press, 1987.

Pohlen, Jerome. *Albert Einstein and Relativity for Kids: His Life and Ideas with 21 Activities and Thought Experiments*. Chicago: Chicago Review, 2012.

## LOUIS ARMSTRONG

Armstrong, Louis. *Louis Armstrong, in His Own Words: Selected Writings*. Oxford: Oxford University Press, 2001.

Bergreen, Laurence. *Louis Armstrong: An Extravagant Life*. New York: Broadway Books, 1997.

Teachout, Terry. *Pops: A Life of Louis Armstrong*. Boston: Houghton Mifflin Harcourt, 2009.

## FRIDA KAHLO

Frida Kahlo: Paintings, Biographies, Quotes. FridaKahlo.org. Accessed October 27, 2021. https:// www.fridakahlo.org/.

Herrera, Hayden. *Frida: The Biography of Frida Kahlo*. London: Bloomsbury, 2018.

Kahlo, Frida. *Diary of Frida Kahlo*. With introduction by Carlos Fuentes, and contributions by Sarah M. Lowe. New York: H. N. Abrams, 1995.

Kahlo, Frida, and John Morrison. *Frida Kahlo*. Philadelphia: Chelsea House, 2003.

## EUGENIE CLARK

Clark, Eugenie. *The Lady and the Sharks*. New York: Harper & Row, 1969.

McGovern, Ann. *Shark Lady: True Adventures of Eugenie Clark*. New York: Scholastic, 1978.

Reis, Ronald A. *Eugenie Clark: Marine Biologist*. New York: Ferguson, 2005.

## AUDREY HEPBURN

Karney, Robyn. *Audrey Hepburn: A Charmed Life*. New York: Arcade, 2017.

Matzen, Robert. *Dutch Girl: Audrey Hepburn and World War II*. Pittsburgh: GoodKnight Books, 2019.

Pepper, Terence, and Helen Trompeteler. *Audrey Hepburn: Portraits of an Icon*. New York: Skira Rizzoli, 2015.

## ROBERTO CLEMENTE

Clemente Museum. Accessed October 27, 2021. https://clementemuseum.com/.

Maraniss, David. *Clemente: The Passion and Grace of Baseball's Last Hero*. New York: Simon & Schuster, 2013.

Volkmer, Jon. *Roberto Clemente: The Story of a Champion*. West Berlin, NJ: Townsend, 2008.

Walker, Paul Robert. *Pride of Puerto Rico: The Life of Roberto Clemente*. San Diego: Harcourt Brace Jovanovich, 1991.

## RAVEN WILKINSON

*Black Ballerina*. Directed by Francis McElroy. Philadelphia: Shirley Road Productions, 2016.

Lansky, Chava Pearl. "Remembering Raven Wilkinson, Trailblazing Ballerina." *Pointe*, December 19, 2018. https://pointemagazine.com/remembering-raven-wilkinson-trailblazing -black-ballerina/.

Schubert, Leda. *Trailblazer: The Story of Ballerina Raven Wilkinson*. New York: Little Bee, 2018.

## BRUCE LEE

Lee, Shannon. *Be Water, My Friend: The Teachings of Bruce Lee*. New York: Flatiron Books, 2020.

Little, John. *Bruce Lee: A Warrior's Journey*. Burbank, CA: Warner Home Video, 2000.

———. *The Warrior Within: The Philosophies of Bruce Lee*. Chicago: Contemporary Books, 1996.

Polly, Matthew. *Bruce Lee: A Life*. London: Simon & Schuster, 2019.

## ANDRÉ THE GIANT

*Andre the Giant*. Directed by Jason Hehir. New York: HBO Sports, 2018. https://www.hbo.com /documentaries/andre-the-giant.

Elwes, Cary, and Joe Layden. *As You Wish: Inconceivable Tales from the Making of* The Princess Bride. New York: Atria Books, 2014.

Hébert, Bertrand, and Pat Laprade. *The Eighth Wonder of the World: The True Story of Andre the Giant*. Toronto: ECW, 2020.

Krugman, Michael. *Andre the Giant: A Legendary Life*. London: Pocket Books, World Wrestling Entertainment, 2009.

# INDEX

# ABOUT THE AUTHOR

Carlyn Beccia (pronounced Betcha) is an author, illustrator, and graphic designer. Beccia's children's books, including *Monstrous*, *The Raucous Royals*, *I Feel Better with a Frog in My Throat*, and *They Lost Their Heads*, have won numerous awards including the Golden Kite Honor, the International Reading Association's Children's and Young Adult Book Award, and the Cybils Award. At the age of ten, Carlyn rode horses at breakneck speeds, sketched monsters, and drove her parents up the wall. The sketching at least worked out. To learn more about her, visit her at www.CarlynBeccia.com.